Umbrella Tree

Selected Poems by

MICHAEL SHERIDAN STONE

twentyfivefiftytwo

To Africa – its landscape, wildlife and, above all, its people

Published by twentyfivefiftytwo

A CIP Catalogue record for this book is available from the British Library.

ISBN 978-1-9996653-7-1

Designed & Typeset by Mark Bracey

Printed in Great Britain.

Contents

Acknowledgements

I have previously recorded my gratitude to a number of friends for their part in the preparation of *The African Sun* and *Matilda visits Luangwa* but one of them merits fresh mention here, namely, Arthur Dunkley, whom I have known since the age of twelve. Arthur is undoubtedly the most sublimely talented individual I have ever met and, fortunately for me, his talents include poetry and photography. He has invested a lot of valuable time in acting as editor of numerous poems in this book and has also contributed the cover photograph of an umbrella tree (*Acacia tortillis*).

I am again indebted to Mark Bracey (twentyfivefiftytwo) for kindly undertaking to publish *Umbrella Tree*.

Foreword

As I have previously stated in the Foreword to my earlier book *The African Sun*, I cannot legitimately call myself a poet. I merely have intermittent poetic impulses that are triggered by episodes and emotions, primarily involving Africa. Although I have lived most of my life in England, I am African in heart, spirit, temperament and voice and I try to get back to the continent as frequently as I can. Unhappily, my travels no longer encompass my former homeland of Zimbabwe, to which I have no intention of returning until the malign influences that still pervade it are spent. But it remains actively in my thoughts and much of my poetry has a Zimbabwean theme.

My poetic output is limited and I have written my poems to satisfy particular needs of my own, rather than with their publication in mind. It was only the encouragement of friends to share the poems with a wider audience that carried me along the publication trail, leading to *The African Sun* in 2009 and *Matilda visits Luangwa* last year. While the urge was still upon me, I felt it appropriate to amalgamate 33 of the poems in those books with eight others that have not previously been published. In making my selection I have decided to omit virtually all of the verses in *The African Sun* that were, in their essence, angry protests against the excesses of the Mugabe regime. Sadly, they are not as 'dated' as I would have wished them to be but I would like this book *Umbrella Tree* to have a less strident feel to it.

Even with this softer approach, I am conscious of difficulties. How can I reasonably expect outsiders to relate to my worship of the African sun and the African bush or the joy of my encounters with elephants, lions, leopards, flufftails and snakes or my deep affection for the African people or my implacable opposition to the tyrants who are blighting their lives? I have provided some notes to explain the context or tone of certain poems, or words or expressions in them, but I appreciate that, at least in part, they may remain somewhat opaque or elusive to those without African affiliations.

The poems are placed in four sections, namely, 'Contemplative', 'African Bush', 'Madagascan' and 'The Owl House' but these sections are not intended to be mutually exclusive. My introduction to each section will provide some background information to certain of the more abstruse poems in that section.

My wish is that something in the poems will strike a chord with you.

Michael Sheridan Stone
London
May 2020

Contemplative Poems

Introduction

Many of the disparate poems in this opening section of the book owe their existence to my contemplation of my own life or the lives of others while resting idly in the Zimbabwean bush or the hills above Barrydale or on the pastures of the South Downs or the lawns of Kew Gardens. Throughout my life I have needed to be outside in order to find any semblance of inventiveness or inspiration.

I spent all of my formative years in Rhodesia (as Zimbabwe then was) and, despite not having lived there for all of five decades, it still claims a special place in my heart - although that heart is now deeply pained by the country's desperate plight.

In 1966 I was fortunate enough to obtain a Rhodes Scholarship to study at Oxford University and left Rhodesia for what turned out to be the final time the following year. When I eventually went back to Salisbury (soon to be Harare) on business in April 1980, the country had been transformed into the newly independent Zimbabwe, with a government of national unity blessed with multiple talents, and tourists were flocking back to the Victoria Falls, game reserves and eastern highland resorts. I had missed thirteen years of UDI (Unilateral Declaration of Independence) and the concomitant international isolation, sanctions and 'war of liberation'. Even after independence not all was sweetness and light; as recorded in the ditty 'Comradeship', there were obvious cracks in the relationship between Mashona and Matabele and these were to deepen, with tragic consequences, during the years ahead.

I became reacquainted with close friends from school, enjoyed the delights of the bush and generally felt I had returned home. But not having shared the pain of the period of strife and armed struggle with my former countrymen, I quickly realised that I did not truly 'belong' and my poem 'Home' records that stark realization, as does 'The African Sun' in a gentler and more whimsical way. The sonnet 'The Search' is a lament for my failure to 'communicate' with my late brother David when I visited his final resting place in the Warren Hills; he died tragically young in 1964.

When I last visited Zimbabwe in October 1998 the country remained a wonderful place for a holiday but the infrastructure was definitely creaking. A few years later commercial farms were invaded by self-styled 'war veterans', laid to waste and rendered totally unproductive. The economy went into steep decline, the key utilities and services crumbled, there were enhanced levels of oppression and corruption, and the quality of life, for all but a privileged few, plummeted to unbelievable depths. The African dream had become a nightmare, as I relate in 'The Distant Drums' and the prospect of 'Closure' draws ever nearer.

Since January 2003 I have travelled to South Africa at regular intervals and have come to know and love the mountain village of Barrydale in the Overberg on the fringes of the Little Karoo. It is a relaxed and tranquil place, mercifully free of the security fences and ferocious dogs that besmirch the more affluent suburbs of South Africa's larger towns. Barrydale is an ideal place to reflect on life, and on your vocation in life, more particularly along one of the less frequented mountain trails that weave their meandering way through the softly coloured fynbos. You may encounter the odd snake (as I recount in 'Interlude' in the next section of the book), although they generally slide away when they hear you coming; this only adds spice to the trek. The greater likelihood – and potential danger – is that you will unwittingly diverge from the trail, as it is all too easy to do, both above Barrydale and in life. At the end of your walk you

can relax and reflect at The Country Pumpkin or The Blue Cow or another of the village's delightful tearooms.
My own journey of intended self-discovery is described in 'The Pumpkin or the Cow'.

I can thoroughly recommend an excursion to an arid enclave known as 'The Manger' that is a short distance from Barrydale. It is the site of what I believe to be Africa's only Buddhist pagoda. Contiguous to that somewhat incongruous landmark is a beautiful labyrinth fringed by pink flowers and demarcated by low walls of rose quartz crystal. If it is open, you can stroll languidly towards its central 'petals', there to sit in welcome shade, and surrender yourself to passive contemplation. The labyrinth merits a poem of its own in this section and it also inspired me to compose 'Umbrella Tree' and 'The Distant Drums'.

I have written very few poems that have no connection whatsoever with Africa and most of those do not merit reproduction. Two that I am including in this book centre upon individuals with whom I never conversed but who nevertheless made a deep and lasting impact upon me.

I have been fortunate enough to enjoy a varied and interesting life and am frequently asked to identify the person who has most impressed me. My answer is consistent and never fails to astonish. It is someone who swept the pavements outside Buckingham Palace, which I walked past for many years on my way to work in Piccadilly from Victoria station. The sweeper was an elderly man who seemed utterly at peace with himself and his environment, oblivious to the throng of tourists who gawped through the Palace railings, and the trusted friend of every bird within earshot. When he emitted a gentle whistle a miscellany of birds flew in from every direction and settled upon his arms and bowed back. Never before or since have I encountered anybody with that degree of affinity to nature. My tribute to him is contained in 'Communion'.

How often does one travel on a train or bus and sit next to or opposite someone for a significant period without learning (or wanting to learn) the first thing about him or her? The answer is probably in about 99.9% of instances. That is certainly my experience. In 'Brief Encounter' I describe the exceptional situation. Regrettably, I have never 'met' the woman in question again as she fascinated me and probably had a compelling story to tell.

The final poem is 'Africa Revisited', which I originally wrote on a postcard from Kenya to a friend in England. As much as my heart lies in Africa and as much as I might dream about living there again, I would miss large elements of my present life in England – the variable weather (surprisingly!), the different seasons, especially the winter, the moors and the South Downs, the wonderful Thames and, most of all, my family and friends. I want to continue to visit different parts of Africa for as long as humanly possible but my days of residing there are past. This takes me rather neatly back to 'The African Sun' at the beginning of this section and to my failure in my advancing years to unleash the blood red ball lodged firmly in my childhood eye.

Additional notes on the poems marked with an asterisk can be found in the Appendix.

The African Sun*

Once I owned a blood red ball
And tossed it high above the hill,
I watched it deftly fall to earth,
And scamper round of its free will.

Above each crest it peeped and winked
And bounded left and chortled right,
It pranced until the darkness came,
Then slithered quickly from my sight.

Each new morning up it rose,
And teased me as I came to play,
It bobbed beyond my stretching arms
And melted gently into day.

It lost all hint of shape and bounce
And vanished in amorphous blue;
Then snubbed me as I strained my eye
To heaven where the eagles flew.

It reappeared late afternoon
And greeted me upon my lawn,
Ducked within my boyish clasp,
And so another game was born.

We played that game for many years,
'Til I grew tired of childish joy,
I closed my mind to lighter whims,
And cast aside my lifelong toy.

I moved afar to sullen climes
Where sun was lost to cloud and rain,
And now that I was growing old
I yearned to find my friend again.

So back I went to Africa,
And gazed intent at cloudless sky;
I watched the sun from dawn to dusk,
Creeping low and perching high;
But though I earned some inner peace,
I found whatever ploy I'd try
Could not unleash that long lost ball,
Lodged firmly in a childhood eye.

Umbrella Tree*

Umbrella tree,
Please welcome me,
Explain how you survive;
You stand alone
Where nothing's grown,
While I am burnt alive.

Umbrella tree,
Please shelter me
From unrelenting sun;
My legs are splayed
In cherished shade;
Salvation has begun.

Umbrella tree,
Please nurture me
With root and leaf and bark;
Just keep me here,
Set free from fear,
Until I greet the dark.

Home*

My dry lips touched the grass of home,
Kissed in joy the sunburnt earth,
Whispered heartfelt words of love
To the land that gave me birth.

I lay at peace in timeless sun,
Gifting warmth from clear blue sky,
Embraced the hills I knew so well,
The little stream that trickled by.

My mind leapt back to carefree youth,
Rued the lost years spent away -
The very years deprived to men
Whose lives were stolen in this vlei[1].

Could that cheeky go-away bird[2],
Chiding me for creeping near,
Once have scolded fighting men,
Seeking refuge from their fear?

Did this stately mukwa[3] tree,
Blessed with magic healing charms,
Cling more tightly to its bark
And shelter strident men at arms?

Did this quietly rustling wind,
Weaving gently through my hair,
Wail and roar and snarl in hate
As slaughter laid the bushveld bare?

Had the auburn grass sprung tall,
Nourished by the unclaimed dead?
Was it some old schoolfriend's blood
That stained the sad msasas[4] red?

What gave the country its allure?
- The sacrifice[5] I never shared;
This land belongs to those who fought,
Not to one whom fortune spared.

1 Marshy land
2 Grey lourie, whose strident call resembles
"Go away!"
3 A species of teak; its bark and roots are used
in traditional medicine to treat a wide variety
of ailments, ranging from malaria to asthma
4 A small shapely tree whose leaves have a
distinctive amber and wine red colour when
the young leaves sprout during spring
5 Although the precise number of lives lost
during the 'war of liberation' in Zimbabwe
will never be known, it is estimated that up to
30,000 people of all races were killed, including
several of my school-friends and teachers.

The Search

I stood alone with you and other
Distant shades, outside my earthly ken,
Yet claiming you as brother,
And sought for you down Time's dark glen,
Past memory of later joy and pain,
To long forgotten days when we were young;
I urged you to appear - in vain,
For I could not use celestial tongue
Or find a wraith with your brief imprint;
No power in me could draw you back
To my vexed mind; the only hint
Of you the staid bronze plaque
That simply states your name and age -
And when you left this mortal stage.

The Labyrinth

The place I seek comes close to reach,
Within the rose quartz labyrinth
That lurks in stark karoo.
The crystal walls shade different paths
That point towards my goal.
I skip along the first,
Filled with boundless hope;
That avenue is quickly blocked
So I must try elsewhere.
The second way seems clearer;
I stroll with faith undimmed,
No barriers in view,
The object of my quest
Is just a touch from here.
Then subtle twists send me
Back to where the path began.
I roar in sheer frustration,
But steel myself once more;
I know which routes I cannot use
And which may take me home.

The Pumpkin or the Cow

I parked my car near Barrydale
To start out on my quest,
Found a well-marked mountain trail
And tackled it with zest.

I strode along with steadfast face,
Weighed what my friends had said,
I needed time and peace and space
To plan the years ahead.

I dwelt upon some well-worn themes,
Forged few things that were new,
Slashed away the wilder dreams,
The path ran straight and true.

Then I came to rocky ground,
My pace dropped to a crawl,
Thoughts were even less profound,
I reached a waterfall.

I slumped to earth a weary man
And all I yearned for now
Was a slice of homemade fruit flan
At the Pumpkin[1] or the Cow[2].

I drank a little from a spring,
Then set off up a slope,
My mind distilled another thing
That gave me future hope.

The trail divided at the top,
My choice the route straight on,
I judged a cherished scheme a flop,
One more illusion gone.

The waymark arrows disappeared
To strand me on a peak;
My addled brain now swiftly cleared,
I scrambled down a creek.

My body took a lot of flak,
I shredded my best shorts,
Large pebbles bruised my aching back,
This stopped all further thoughts.

I rested under cloudless sky
And wondered if somehow
I could have a homemade meat pie
At the Pumpkin or the Cow.

I crossed a tangled, shallow ditch
And came out on some tar,
Then Fate unfurled a further glitch,
I couldn't find my car.

I dragged my wounded, cramping legs
Through tangled bush and fern,
A thicket full of barbs and pegs
That thwarted every turn.

Six times I fell into a brook,
Then pulled myself upright,
I suffered pain each step I took
But won this final fight.

Now my journey reached its end
With two key lessons learned:
Courage is your truest friend
And what means most is earned.

Survival, life's one timeless art,
Inspired my joyous vow -
To celebrate with milk tart[3]
At the Pumpkin or the Cow.

1 The Country Pumpkin tearoom in Barrydale
2 The Blue Cow tearoom in Barrydale
3 A traditional (and delicious!) South African
  dessert

Hills

We pant our way
Up sun-baked slopes
And feel no need for speech.
The dusty path has ushered thought
Of greener hills
Through which we roamed
Before our lives were clamped;
Of friendship forged in callow years
From which we've long since fled.
When I can loosen my constraints,
I hasten to these parts,
Where you await my call;
Our bond remains secure,
Defying vanished time.
Soon this path will reach its end
And I will leave these hills;
I'll give my promise to return,
Knowing you'll be there.

The Peregrine

Suddenly I broke away and lived;
My soul touched sky
And soared untrammelled
To the beckoning sun.

I sped alone beyond the earth,
Remote from man's gaunt bond,
And, spreading wing, exalted
In the joy of silent poise.

My perfect pitch awakened
Fresh knowledge of myself;
I gloried in the cadence
Of unremitting flight.

Then I saw a doleful dove,
Who had no sense of doom above;
Down I plunged
And stooped and lunged.

I ripped and tore
With beak and claw,
Immersed myself in flesh and gore,
Feasting high but wanting more.

The bird's sweet essence entered me,
Infusing me with love,
My transient day flushed crimson
In homage to the dove.

I hovered softly in repose,
Then, drifting idly back to ground,
Gripped the gloved hand.
Thus embraced, I died.

Through their Eyes

They play a game
That we once played
Some fifty years ago;
A dusty field,
An ancient ball,
Two teams of ragged youths,
Who run and kick,
Laugh and shout,
And dream of future fame.
Our fondest hopes
Were stifling lies
That kept us in our place,
But theirs can soar unchecked.
Their joyous whoops
Become diffuse,
Then scatter in the air;
Yet this uplifting message
Shines out crystal clear;
They control their destiny –
I hear it through their eyes.

The Distant Drums

There was a time of dread and fear,
When man went out with gun or spear
To right the wrongs of yesteryear,
In Africa[1].

The battles raged a long, long time,
With streams to cross and hills to climb,
And men sank deep in gore and grime,
In Africa.

And in the distance harsh drums beat
A ruthless rhythm for bare feet.

Countless people died in pain,
Black and white among the slain;
When would peace break out again,
In Africa?

Then at last an end to strife,
With prospects of more normal life,
Surviving men could take a wife,
In Africa.

And in the distance proud drums beat
A rousing rhythm for quick feet.

The wasted years left much to do,
A new regime would see things through,
This was what it promised you,
In Africa.

All the kids were now at school,
A tribute to emergent rule,
This land would be the shining jewel,
Of Africa.

And in the distance soft drums beat
A gentle rhythm for shod feet.

The leaders rode in smart new cars,
Drank their tea from cups, not jars,
They might as well have lived on Mars,
Not Africa.

They lost their focus due to greed
And quite forgot the people's need
To build more homes and plant more seed,
In Africa.

And in the distance sad drums beat
A forlorn rhythm for tired feet.

The people grew extremely poor,
No work on farms or factory floor,
With AIDS a scourge for ever more,
In Africa.

Flimsy shacks were bulldozed down[2]
By soldiers paid to cleanse the town
Of human filth of no renown,
In Africa.

The people had no more to give,
Few mealie[3] cobs were left to sieve,
They've almost lost the will to live,
In Africa.

And now the distant drums were stilled
As all grand hopes and dreams were killed,
In Africa.

1 Specifically Zimbabwe, although the history
described will have echoes in other African
countries
2 A well publicized ruthless episode that was
designed to destabilize opponents of President
Robert Mugabe
3 Maize or corn

Comradeship

How can you be my brother
When you are not like me?
I'm from here, you're from there;
We think quite differently.

We cannot march together;
It is futile to pretend
That I will call you comrade,
For you are not my friend.

Closure

Turn off your tap, redundant rain,
There's nothing left to grow,
Let drought pervade this stark domain
'Til shoots of justice show.

Blow yourself out, unhelpful wind,
The stench of death can lurk,
Let stillness swamp the men who've sinned
'Til screams of protest work.

Switch off your light, unwelcome sun,
While madmen stalk this land,
Let darkness stay 'til we've begun
To touch bright freedom's hand.

Communion

He stoops and finds God on the pavement,
Among the dutiful feet
That trudge towards the Palace[1],
In tired pursuit of splendour.
His hand-hewn brush dispels a clod
That might offend the welling herd:
He hums a simple tune
To summon varied friends.

His wealth transcends all other in that crowd,
For he is Nature's serf and king,
An ancient child untouched by care of time,
Whose soul communes with the distant sky,
With the smallest bird on the humblest tree.
He holds his world in a gnarled brown hand,
A trusted palm where sparrows lightly fuss
And bid spry welcome to a reverential thrush,
Who trills in unashamed delight
A hymn of praise upon the altar
Of the old man's cambered back.

Some languid doves swell the throng
Of worshippers and worshipped,
And feed upon the greying crusts
The veteran draws from dusty pockets;
No shallow words will spoil
The silent bond of Nature with this man.
He bends once more to chat with God.

1 Buckingham Palace in London

Brief Encounter

We met on the tube[1]
At Baker Street[2];
Eight o'clock.
You sat next to me
Or I sat next to you,
No matter which.
You wore a stylish skirt
And diamond ring;
Hair cut short,
With fringe,
No lustre.
You never looked at me
But I saw you;
Dismay
Etched in your face,
Not pretty
Yet still a bit
Attractive.
Fingers clenched,
Clasping bag,
Staring into space;
You pinched your lip,
Sucked your thumb
Like a child;
But what child looks
So tired and drawn,
And full of sorrow?
You closed your eyes,
Heavy lids,
Shadowed,
Lined with worry;
Scratched your nose
And sighed;

A pensive sound
That only we could hear.
You chewed your nails,
Twice,
Rubbed your mouth,
Cupped your chin
In your hand.

What troubled you:
Man or job
Or debt
Or life itself?
I cared but never knew;
You never knew I cared.
We exited at Charing Cross[3]
At eight ten.
You first,
Then me behind;
Shared the escalator
To the top.
You left me.

1 The vernacular name for a train on the London
underground system
2 A station on the London Underground
3 Another station on the London Underground

Angels of the Snow

They mock the verdant wasteland
that is Kew –
the unrelenting green
of trees and shrubs
and dormant bulbs
that wait in vain
for warmer days to come.

They dance above the frost-flecked grass;
one hundred heads
of pastel blue
sway to the rhythm
of the whistling wind
on a carpet made
of fallen petals.

They shimmer in the winter sun;
a final burst of glory
as their colour
starts to fade
on wilting stems
and they melt
into nothing.

Africa Revisited

The harsh sun bakes my addled mind
And burns away my childhood dream
To venture far to Europe
And beyond.
That dream is long fulfilled -
But I am unfulfilled.

Now I yearn for Africa again;
Parched hills and plains,
Squat trees,
And multitudes of animals and birds
Too numerous
For anyone to name;
BUT…
I would sorely miss
My friends like you!

African Bush Poems

Introduction

I have an abiding passion for the African bush and its wildlife -
mammals, birds and reptiles alike: I can do without most of the
insects! This passion had its origin in a short visit that I made
with my father to the newly opened Luangwa National Park in
Zambia when I was aged just twelve. I lost my heart to countless
elephant, giraffe, zebra, buffalo, kudu and eland and recoiled in
fear at hippo, hyena and crocodile. Lion and leopard eluded us
but I would eventually catch up with them during later trips to
game reserves.

Perhaps the most memorable of those trips occurred in 2015 when
I made a long-deferred return visit to Luangwa, accompanied
by my younger daughter Nicola and my grandchildren Harrison
and Matilda. By coincidence Matilda was exactly the same age
(twelve) as I was when I first set foot in this amazing national
park. Matilda had close encounters with hippo, crocodile, leopard,
buffalo, porcupine, hyena, elephant and a lion pride and enjoyed
other eye-popping experiences. The story of her trip has been
distilled in narrative, poems, sketches and photographs in a book
entitled "Matilda visits Luangwa", to which I contributed 20
poems. Half of them are reproduced in this section of "Umbrella
Tree"; they are joined by six others that originally appeared in
"The African Sun" and a previously unpublished poem called
'Chapungu', which might easily have found a place in the first
section of this book, as it is highly 'contemplative'! It also calls for
quite a lot of explanation and I have sought to provide this both in
detailed footnotes to the poem and in a supplementary note in the
Appendix. There is also a supplementary note on the Elephants
trilogy but I believe that the remaining 'African Bush' poems do
not need any particular elaboration.

*Additional notes on the poems marked with an asterisk can be found
in the Appendix.*

First Love

I sat above a river bank
And scoured the bush around,
Searching for some creatures
To make my young heart pound.

I watched hyena grin and lope,
Some buck and warthog too,
But all of them flew out of mind
The moment I saw you.

You lounged below me on a rock,
Lit by the morning sun,
Your beauty took my breath away,
I begged you not to run.

You wore a finely tailored coat
That stretched from head to paw,
Coloured cream with dark black spots
No human hand could draw.

I looked into your amber eyes,
They stared intently back,
You had a regal quality
That other females lack.

Your sharp white teeth flashed me a smile,
You growled some sounds of bliss,
I hankered to get close to you
But feared your deadly kiss.

Then you rose and walked at pace
Beside the sunlit stream,
I waved my hand in sad farewell
And saw your whiskers gleam.

You gazed at me one final time,
Then left me there above,
I never have forgotten you,
You[1] were my first true love.

1 For those who have not yet guessed,
   the subject of the poem is a leopard!

Interlude

I thought it quite polite to greet
My neighbour on the rock;
He lay there in the scorching sun,
Curled up in a block.

I moved a step along the path,
Intent to call "Good Day";
My neighbour raised his awesome head
Just fifteen feet away.

He started to uncoil himself,
His movement was so smooth;
I checked the greeting in my throat
And made a backward move.

His length grew greater all the time,
Or so it seemed to me,
His jet black presence held me rapt
And froze me on the scree.

My mind distilled an ancient myth,
The serpent tempting Eve,
For I was drawn towards the snake[1],
And had no wish to leave.

The snake was king in this domain
And he would make the choice -
To send me silent from his hill,
Or let me have my voice.

1 Cape cobra

He peered at me through narrowed lids,
His tongue flicked to and fro;
It seemed unlikely we'd be friends;
I judged it best to go.

I scrambled down the slope I'd climbed
And bade the snake farewell;
It was a stirring interlude -
And one more tale to tell.

The Reluctant Baboon

"Come along, big boy;
Time to go",
An anxious voice is hailing me.
But I don't want to leave this tree;
I join my friends and leap around,
Taunting my mother on the ground:
"You'll never catch me,
You're too slow!"

"Hurry to me;
Do as you're told";
My mouth is full of luscious fig,
I'm feasting like a greedy pig;
There's still no way I'm jumping down,
I pull a face and act the clown:
"You'll never catch me;
You're too old!"

"Listen to me!
You horrid brat!
It's getting dark and you must come";
I yawn out loud, display my gum,
Descend at pace and skip away:
"Don't hassle me, I want to stay;
You'll never catch me:
You're too fat!"

"Your mother's soft but I am not!":
A massive voice is booming near;
Huge hands grasp me by each ear;
My father gives my head a shake
And drags me squealing in his wake;
A spanking makes my backside hot!

Visit to a Pool

I'd dive in head first as a rule,
The quickest way to make me cool;
Should I do this I'd be a fool;
A crocodile lies in the pool
Today.

The pool contains a crocodile,
Six feet long with toothy smile;
He'll surely cramp my swimming style;
I think instead I'll run a mile
Away.

Four Little Warthogs

Out of the burrow, quickly now,
You have to learn to feed somehow;
No more mother's milk for you,
You must find something you can chew;
Heads low down, look for shoots,
The tender type that sprout from roots;
When you kneel down and start to dig
Remember carnivores eat pig;
All four of you must stay in line,
Stick close together, you'll be fine;
If you sense danger, sound alarm,
I'll keep you safe from any harm;
Your upright tails will serve as flags -
And woe betide the one who lags!

The Shy Bushbuck

I marvel that you live as long as you do
When so many factors conspire against you;
Your fawn-coloured body looks flimsy and frail,
Delicate spots mark your neck, legs and tail,
Innocuous horns and a cute little hump,
You've no penchant to run tho' you swim and you jump;
You cannot resist or escape an attack
But do possess something that stronger beasts lack;
You can be on your own without limit of time,
Stay hidden from view yet not burrow or climb;
Standing perfectly still in thickets of bush,
Protected by branches, or thorns at a push,
Your camouflage helps to keep hunters away;
Needing little to eat or drink in a day,
You are seldom inclined to venture too far -
Seclusion is certainly your lucky star.

Transience

A shimmering blanket floats down from the sky,
Draping green folds on a well-berried bush;
It tears into shreds as a hawk hovers high,
Two hundred lovebirds erupt with a whoosh.

Pel's Fishing Owl

Can you really, truly, be
The rarest bird I'll ever see?
You should be very hard to find
(And, if you were, I wouldn't mind)
But you sit here in open view
Like routine birds, not something new;
You dominate the starlit night,
No twigs or brush to block my sight;
You make no move to fly away;
I pray that you'll prolong your stay,
Absorbing details while I can.

It seems your wings have endless span;
The power that made you did not stint –
Your bulky frame of ginger tint
Is two feet long at least, I think;
Large dark eyes that seldom blink
Stare idly at our little group;
You give a gently muffled whoop.

Then at last it's time to go,
You take your leave with little show;
I can't believe I've seen and heard
Pel's Fishing Owl – the rarest bird.

Leopard Cub at Bay

Twelve small strides, just twelve small strides, until I'm safe at last;
I'm a tiny leopard cub who cannot move too fast.
My mother should be guarding me but she's gone off somewhere;
There's now a big cat stalking me – she doesn't seem to care.
I don't know who this stranger is, I've not seen him before;
I can't look back but always hear the sound of stealthy paw.
I really need my mother now – where can the old girl be?
She can't be far from this loved spot; this is our own home tree.
I clamber up the sturdy trunk, the big male lurks below;
If I should stumble, worse still fall, there'll be a tale of woe.
My claws are sharp and I go up, beyond his lengthy reach;
I shiver on my favourite branch and give a plaintive screech.
A sudden movement in a bush, my mother's on her way;
She sees the leopard hounding me and speeds across the vlei[1].
The trespasser takes to his heels, Mother's closing in,
A missile tearing through the night, she makes my small head spin.
She snarls and snaps her fearsome jaws to aid him in his flight;
I sit at peace astride my branch and I'll sleep well tonight.

---

1 Marshy land

The Lone Hyena

The starlight fades: Luangwa greets the dawn;
Those who dwell in darkness fall asleep.
Little stirs to start the new-born day –
But one relentless prowler's
Still at large.

He leers, then scowls, then grins in turn,
Plods along a rutted track;
Unhurried, scanning front and back, left and right,
In search of trifles,
Whether live or lately dead.

He shakes his mane of tousled hair and cackles,
A ghoulish sound that echoes through the bush,
Fraying nerves of small nocturnal things
Who catch the scent of killer on patrol
And scurry into cover.

He's ventured out alone, no others
Claiming shares in what he finds;
His enemies are few, save lions.
But there's no sign of any cats today
So he can roam at will.

He crouches, ever watchful, near a stream,
Rinses last night's meal from stubby teeth,
Then laughs aloud in unremitting glee.
His sloping back falls out of view;
He hurries to his lair.

On Guard

Ebbing sun marks the end of the day;
Six sprightly puku are stopping their play.
Now is the time we must be on our guard,
Surviving the night can be terribly hard.
I see a large shape at the foot of a mound –
A lion's around…yes, a lion's around!

There's safety in numbers, we're taught to believe:
We must keep together and no-one must leave.
The six of us here seem clamped in a net,
Each puku committed to watching for threat.
I sense the swift flick of an elegant ear –
Lions are near…yes, lions are near!

Twelve eyes transfixed by the danger at hand:
While others might flee, we determine to stand.
Our courage is fragile, we bolster our will
And trust that the hunters aren't anxious to kill.
I detect the soft twitch of a long feline nose –
Nervousness grows…yes, nervousness grows.

Darkness is falling, we should hasten away
But if lions sense movement we'll be easy prey.
Everyone knows that we're brave and we're strong,
Against these cruel monsters we seldom last long.
Fate intervenes and they wander away –
It's our lucky day…yes, our lucky day!

Elephants*

Have you played with elephants?
If not, you've missed some fun;
Settle gently in your chair,
I'll tell you how it's done;
Choose a smart camp on a hill,
Remote in Hwange Park[1],
Stroll around the bush all day,
Then wander back at dark;
Light a fire to have a braai[2],
Open up cold beers,
Let the moonlight wash your face
And rinse away your fears;
Prepare to hear the tallest tales,
Then tell some of your own,
Why honey badgers[3] strike the groin,
How loud their victims moan;
Have another beer or two,
Eat some wors[4] and steak,
Stretch out on the luscious grass,
Give your mind a break.

Lift your eyes in wonderment
As elephants trudge in,
Past the braai and past yourself,
Ten metres from your chin;
You never hear them on the move,
They walk as if on foam,
Gliding from the distant bush
To this, their second home;
They drink from leaky water pipes
That make the grass grow green;
They mill around, ignoring you,
Though you've been clearly seen;

You want to take some backward steps,
But you are held transfixed,
Mighty beasts loll everywhere,
Bulls and youths all mixed;
Tusks are flashing near your fire,
Trunks are intertwined,
The elephants are playing games
With any toys they find.

You decide you're not a toy,
Resolve to rest your head,
But there are eighteen elephants
Between you and your bed;
They show no sign of bowing out,
So what are you to do?
Take a further beer in hand,
It's time to think things through;
Stride towards the animals
That block your bed-bound path,
Ask them please to step aside,
Almost hear them laugh;
Raise your voice a notch or two,
Holler in their ear,
Clank beer cans incessantly,
Push them in the rear;
Gentle giants dance aside,
Let you through their ranks,
You have played with elephants,
For which give hearty thanks.

1 A game reserve in the western part of Zimbabwe quite close to
   the Victoria Falls
2 Barbecue
3 Also known as the ratel. It is similar in size and shape to the European
   badger and is widely regarded as the fiercest animal in the African bush
4 Boerewors, a traditional South African sausage, that tastes best when
   barbecued and eaten outside

More Elephants*

Have you slept with elephants?
I have, but just with one;
Listen to me for a while,
I'll tell you how it's done;
Take the hottest day you've known,
Start a gruelling trek[1],
Strip off all the clothes you donned,
Tie them round your neck;
Sweat your way along a gorge,
Bathe in every pool,
Cling to any scrap of shade,
Keep your forehead cool;
Plaster on the tanning oil,
Feel your bare skin bake,
Watch klipspringer[2] bound uphill,
Dodge the odd sand snake;
Then at last your due reward,
Taitas[3] flying free,
Speeding low across the cliffs,
The rarest birds you'll see.

1 A long arduous journey, in this case on foot
2 An extremely agile small antelope
3 Taita falcons, which are among Africa's rarest and most elusive birds

Elated by the taitas' flight,
Tramp back down the trail,
Time to choose a spot to sleep
Away from rock and shale;
Clamber stiffly up a slope,
Pant from constant thirst,
Gasp for breath each step you take,
Think your lungs must burst;
Halfway up the endless hill,
Find a spacious cave,
Vaulted roof and sandy floor,
The refuge that you crave;
Start to move your clobber[4] in,
Hear the whine of bees,
Hurl yourself below the swarm,
Crawl out on your knees;
On and upwards still you go,
Then you strike the top,
Reach a glade of albidas[5],
Decide that's where you'll stop.

4 Clothing and personal items
5 A species of acacia tree, the fruits/pods of which are an important component of the diets of large antelope, buffalo and elephant

Relax at last as darkness falls,
Light your small gas hob,
Cook your meat and beans and pap[6],
Mealies[7] on the cob;
Rest your weary, aching limbs,
Free your mind from doubt,
Put your Qantas eyeshades[8] on,
Block the moonlight out;
Sink into untroubled sleep,
Then hear a crackling sound,
Gently ease your eyeshades off
To see what's on the ground;
An elephant is sidling close,
As quietly as can be,
Intent on chewing tasty pods
He's stripping off a tree;
The animal has come in peace,
So shut your eyes and snore,
You have slept with elephant(s);
How can you ask for more?

6 A solid maize meal paste, rather like white polenta
7 Maize or corn
8 These were a particularly villainous shade of red!

Elephants Again*

Have you swum with elephants?
I nearly did, my son;
If you want to follow me,
I'll tell you how it's done;
Make your way to Mana Pools[1],
Burned russet by the drought,
Trample through the arid bush,
Throw inhibition out;
Fetch a trusted old canoe,
Start your trip downstream,
Trail a line behind the boat,
Try to catch some bream;
Sink a beer Zimbabwe style,
Tilt your head and pour,
Kick your legs until it's drained,
Then go back for more;
Chew some biltong[2] or droewors[3],
Get your salt intake,
Paddle harder for a while,
Earn a short smoke break.

1 A magical game reserve adjoining the Zambezi River
  above Lake Kariba in Zimbabwe
2 Strips of dried venison or beef
3 Dried sausage

Prepare to face some further pain,
Oil yourself and fry,
Hippos lurk among the reeds
But let you safely by;
Join up with the other boats,
Legs will lock them tight,
Time means nothing in the bush,
Drift for your delight;
Jacanas[4] trot on lily leaves,
Carmines[5] dart from banks,
Cheer as stately saddlebills[6]
Dominate greenshanks[7];
Shake off all your lethargy,
Row at breakneck pace,
Steer at every stump and arch,
Win each hard fought race;
Hit a basking crocodile,
Feel it lift your boat,
Pray to all the river gods,
Come back down afloat.

4 A small elegant wading bird; unusually, the male rears
the young
5 Carmine bee-eaters
6 Saddlebill storks, the largest riverine birds at Mana Pools
7 Medium size wading birds that are also found
throughout Europe

Stop beneath a sloping bank,
Shed your shirt and shoes,
Climb into a sandy cove,
Sluice the soiled canoes;
Zambezi glimmers in the sun,
Mana's to the fore,
Fill your lungs with Africa,
Knock at heaven's door;
Elephants arrive unheard,
Five big bulls plod down,
Spray themselves with cooling mud,
Start to play the clown;
Find yourself five yards from them,
Mark their every sound,
Sidle back a foot or two,
Turn the boats around;
Jumbos now decide to drink,
Time to move away;
You've almost swum with elephants,
That's surely made your day.

The Final Journey

One last hunt – one final quest:
Grey and gaunt, all skin and bone,
A lioness in name alone;
She hugs the path that she knows best.

Once the queen of all her pride,
A matriarch both fierce and bold,
She led the chase for years untold -
Until the fire within her died.

She's now too slow to set the traps,
Last one in the feeding line;
Must wait her turn while others dine -
Then nibble some unwanted scraps.

She hears a distant puku bleat,
The other lions sense their prey –
They snarl at her to move away;
She slinks aside in sad retreat.

The pride comes back but she is late:
Savanna grass conceals her fate.

The Silence of the Veldt

Creeping out at first light,
A clamour in my ear,
Birds of all descriptions
Singing loud and clear,
I marvel at the joyous din
That greets the break of day;
Young impala prance about
And infant warthogs play.
Then noise is cruelly shattered,
A creature's doom is spelt,
There's the sound of utter silence -
The silence of the veldt.

Melting in the harsh sun,
My nerves severely frayed,
Animals now well dispersed
In search of scanty shade,
I stagger blindly through the bush
To flop down on the ground;
The cloying heat saps energy
And blankets out all sound.
Oppression takes a stifling grip
That tightens like a belt;
I touch a wall of silence -
The silence of the veldt.

Crouching at a waterhole
Towards the end of day,
Creatures taking final drinks
Before they slip away,
I smell deep fear in animals
Who may not live for long,
The stench of rotting carcases
Is suffocating song.
The grassland reeks of pungent dung
Where buffalo have dwelt;
These odours seal the silence -
The silence of the veldt.

Sprawled beside a camp fire,
A Castle[1] in my hand,
The birds no longer singing
And peace across the land,
I wonder why this is the time
When beers are at their best,
Even though they're warm and flat
And lack their usual zest.
It's not the content of the brew
That makes my taste buds melt,
But the flavour of the silence -
The silence of the veldt.

Sleeping by a bush trail
Where albidas² abound,
My colleagues snoring gently,
No other hint of sound,
I sense the spectre of a beast
Steal near with ghostly tread;
An elephant is chewing pods
Ten metres from my head.
My eyes reveal it standing there
As quiet as if it knelt,
It symbolises silence -
The silence of the veldt.

1 A leading brand of beer in southern Africa
2 A species of acacia tree, the fruits/pods of
   which are an important component of the
   diets of large antelope, buffalo and elephant

Chapungu*

As you settle to sleep you can feel the light touch
Of Chapungu[1] perched soft on your brow;
In the gentlest of tones it will whisper how much
You must yearn to return there somehow,
To a gorge that you trekked[2] with young Arthur and such,
And it's willing to take you right now.

It will loosen the veil that has shrouded the light
From those African days of your past,
And will quietly cajole you to join it in flight
On its mystical wings beating fast;
Through the glittering stars you traverse the dark night,
Then get back to your homeland at last.

When Chapungu alights at a well trodden spot
You are glad that you gave it your trust;
It discloses a kopje[3] you've long since forgot,
With its camp site enveloped in dust,
Where the slats of the cabin have crumbled with rot
And the roof is now burnished by rust.

1 'Chapungu' is the name that the Shona people give to the eagle
called the bateleur, which is French for tightrope walker or
tumbler (the bird has a curious flight pattern in which it is forever
balancing its wings) and which has a great significance in Shona
culture. The bateleur or chapungu is a good omen, the symbol of a
protective spirit and a messenger of the gods. The fabled Zimbabwe
bird found at the Zimbabwe Ruins is considered to be a depiction
of chapungu and is believed to be an ancestral link to the heavens.
It is sometimes called Shiri ya Mwari, the Bird of God. The stone
eagle became the country's emblem and symbol of freedom
because it linked the Shona to their ancient ancestors

2 Hiked arduously

3 Rocky hill

It was somewhere near here that you lay in soft sand
While you mused on green valleys below;
You were living a dream in that magical land
Where your spiritual essence could flow;
Now Chapungu beside you is gripping your hand
And is spurring your ego to grow.

So you shrug off the years and cast caution aside
When you find a familiar trail;
Each endurance technique you possess is applied
As you battle your way through the shale;
You arrive at a krans[4] where all plant-life has died,
Where the spoor[5] of the creatures is stale.

Though the scream of a dikkop[6] will rip through the air
And a klipspringer[7] bound up a slope,
The escarpment you loved has been cruelly laid bare,
Low rainfall means Nature can't cope;
You will pray for fresh life for a treasure so rare
But there's little to stimulate hope.

4 Ridge
5 Identifying marks
6 A weird looking bird very much like the stone curlew
  that visits the UK
7 A small and extremely agile antelope

It is hard to believe that the taita[8] you saw
May yet breed in that deep hidden cleft;
You will listen in vain for a lion to roar
And the kudu[9] and sable[10] have left;
Your companions of old can support you no more
And their absence has made you bereft.

All the rhino you witnessed are butchered and dead
And the vervets[11] can no longer play;
What needs to be told has already been said:
There is nothing to lengthen your stay;
When you wake with a start you're alone in your bed
And Chapungu has melted away.

8 A small, elegant falcon, one of the rarest birds in Africa
9 A large and majestic antelope
10 Another large and majestic antelope
11 Cute and playful monkeys

Madagascan Poems

Introduction

Madagascar, the world's fourth largest island, lies in the
Indian Ocean a few hundred miles from the African
mainland. Very little from the mainland has penetrated,
or even infiltrated, there, which is both a delight and a
disappointment to me. A delight because virtually everything
you see or touch or taste is different, and, in a good many
cases, unique, and a disappointment because Madagascar
almost totally lacks the element of menace that makes
journeys to the wilder parts of Africa so stimulating.
Madagascar is not altogether without its dangers – the steep,
rocky, vine-strewn trails demand extreme care – but, the odd
crocodile or scorpion apart, none of its natural inhabitants is
equipped to inflict significant harm upon you, not even the
myriad snakes, spiders and creepy crawlies. Lions, leopards,
cheetahs and even servils would sneer at Madagascar's only
mammalian predator, the fossa, which preys upon rotund
birds and small lemurs.

The lemurs are an undiluted joy. The most intriguing of them,
as well as being the largest, are the indri; these endearing
animals live in small family groups in dense rain forest and
communicate through harmonized song with neighbouring
families, often a mile or more distant. Predominant among
the other mammals are the zebu, ubiquitous hump-backed
cattle introduced from India, which are to be found in
abundance everywhere outside the protected forest areas.

The above themes and subjects are developed further in
the poems 'Madagascar', 'The Indri' and 'Zebu' that follow.
'The Flufftail' records the pursuit of an elusive bird in the
magnificent Ranomafana National Park under the expert
tutelage of Fidi, one of life's great characters and a veritable
'one-off' among guides. It is a cautionary tale, one that will

be familiar to birdwatchers anywhere in the world. Another elusive bird was the Helmet Vanga. Although I only had a fleeting glimpse of it in its entirety, I did spend a mesmerising 30 minutes in a ditch admiring its magnificent blue bill which was perched enticingly on the ridge of its large nest.

Madagascar is at once a naturalist's greatest delight and his or her worst nightmare. It has a matchless variety of fauna and flora but over 90% of the original acreage of forest (which covered virtually the entire island) has been slashed, burned or otherwise destroyed by man during the span of a few centuries to make temporary way for agriculture, principally to create rice paddies and impoverished pastures for zebu. It is temporary because the land that has been cleared has retreated rapidly into desert. Fortunately, there has been an active programme to preserve as much as possible of the surviving forest and numerous national parks and special reserves have been established. I describe the rapid environmental decline of the once pristine island in 'The Frigatebird', the mighty flyer of that name being to all appearances a survivor from prehistoric times.

In addition to the despoliation of its landscape, Madagascar witnessed unspeakable violations of human dignity in its darker years. The slave trade flourished there, as I recount in 'Black Rocks'; more detailed notes are contained in the Appendix.

All in all, despite its imperfections, Madagascar is magical and I would love to return there.

Madagascar

You broke from old Gondwanaland[1] and drifted out to sea,
Devised the strangest island life that there could ever be,
Spurning tall savannah grass[2] you sprouted forest-tree;
You're not the drought-torn Africa where death strikes constantly:
You are…
Madagascar!

You culled the violent carnivores that ripped their prey apart,
Filtered out large animals and bid them all depart,
Your gentle lemurs prancing round now melt the hardest heart;
You'll never be harsh Africa where carnage is an art:
You are…
Madagascar!

You once had great birds ten feet tall[3] but they're no longer found,
The species you replaced them with are mainly short and round,
Seldom spreading wing to fly they creep along the ground;
You're not the vibrant Africa where fearsome hawks abound:
You are…
Madagascar!

You had no place for deadly snakes and cast them all aside,
Introduced some harmless herps[4] that only want to hide,
Melting into leaves and bark they might as well have died;
You cannot be the Africa where reptiles prowl with pride:
You are…
Madagascar!

You blew out all volcano smoke a million years ago,
Left a trail of tsingi[5] rock that marked the lava flow,
Nothing gaining access there will find the means to grow;
You still don't boast the killer-scapes that Africa can show:
You are…
Madagascar!

Your people never took to maize however low the price,
Stripped away most forest growth and planted fields of rice,
Seeking flavour for their food they cultivated spice[6];
I wish you could be Africa but you are far too nice:
You are…
Madagascar!

1 A huge supercontinent that covered most of the Southern
    Hemisphere about 200 million years ago
2 Tall, bronze grass that grows in much of mainland Africa
3 Notably the "elephant bird" which became extinct at about the
    same time as the dodo and was reputedly the largest bird known
    to the modern world
4 Vernacular term for reptiles and amphibians, including
    chameleons, geckos, lizards and snakes
5 Sharp-edged limestone, extensive in area, that is difficult
    to traverse
6 Madagascar provides the world with a great variety of spices,
    including cinnamon, nutmeg and cloves

The Flufftail

We'd spent the day at 'Fana[1]
With Fidi as our guide,
Scooting up the matted slopes
Then down the other side;
I thought we looked for lemurs,
But that was my mistake,
For Fidi sought a flufftail
As we foundered in his wake.

I've seen a lot of couas[2],
Some rails[3] and vangas[4] too;
But what the hell's a flufftail,
Is it black or brown or blue?

We scrambled into forest,
Through tangled vines and roots,
Ignored the soaring raptors
And lemurs munching shoots;
With Fidi always leading,
His head bent to the ground,
We tried to find a flufftail
(Reluctant to be found).

I've seen some owls and herons,
An oxylabes[5] too;
But what the hell's a flufftail,
Would I know it if it flew?

We stopped at last in silence
As Fidi cupped his hand;
He piped a mournful melody
That echoed through the land;
From deep within the forest
A sombre bird replied,
We'd heard a distant flufftail
And Fidi puffed with pride.

I've seen a mass of fodies[6],
Ground-rollers[7] at nightfall;
But what the hell's a flufftail,
Is it large or squat or small?

The flufftail ventured closer,
Or so friend Fidi said,
To me its call seemed fainter
And I turned away my head;
Fidi dragged me back again,
He leapt high in the air,
His finger started stabbing,
"It's there! It's there! It's there!"

I traced the pointing finger
And looked low in a tree;
Where the hell's the flufftail?
Where can the damn thing be?

Fidi waved his arms about,
His anger was profound,
"The flufftail's right in front of you,
It's walking on the ground!"
He clasped me by the elbow
And pulled me to his side,
But still I couldn't find it,
No matter how I tried.

"Too late! Too late!" screamed Fidi,
"It's disappeared from view";
So what the hell's a flufftail,
Is it brown or black or blue?

1 Ranomafana National Park
2 Species of Madagascan bird, most members of
   which are found nowhere else in the world
3 As **2** above
4 As **2** above
5 As **2** above
6 As **2** above
7 As **2** above

The Indri

Lead me to the indri[1], please,
I want to hear them sing;
Guide me up the forest trails
To where they launch their soulful wails
That call to mind the grisly tales
Of harpies[2] on the wing.

Let me stand beneath the trees
And wait for them to move;
They leap from any spindly bough,
Find a spot to land somehow,
Shriek a hearty high-pitched vow
Their timing will improve.

Help me choose the closest place
To view them while they stay;
They look benign as cuddly toys,
Bicker like young girls and boys,
Take delight in simple joys
Of children at their play.

Tell me when they'll have the grace
To burst into their song;
I thought they'd start up by this time,
But all they've done is act in mime,
Perhaps this group is past its prime
Or been awake too long.

THE INDRI

Hold me as I crane my head
To watch them climb up high;
A chorus has begun to flower,
It rises with an awesome power
To make the bravest creatures cower
And lesser beings cry.

Keep me here until I'm dead,
This is my greatest prize;
Adult tenors fuel the choir,
Young sopranos drive them higher,
Their voices never seem to tire
And proudly harmonize.

Assure me they'll descend anon,
Those lemurs are so quaint;
I'll tolerate a long delay,
It's still quite early in the day,
They cannot be too far away -
No, their carolling grows faint.

Console me now they've been and gone,
It is the saddest thing;
I fell in love right from the start,
Those gorgeous creatures stole my heart,
But now the time has come to part;
I've heard the indri sing.

1 Largest of the living lemurs
2 In Greek and Roman mythology, these were
   monsters with a woman's head and body and
   a bird's wings and claws

The Helmet Vanga

You loiter low within your nest,
Nine parts of you unseen;
What hidden splendours will you flaunt
When you arise to preen?

I've travelled nearly half the world
To catch this glimpse of you,
A single feature peeking out,
Arched bill of cyan blue.

The bill parades a wondrous casque,
A dazzling, vivid cone,
Great toucans would be proud to claim
Your helmet as their own.

Keen yellow eye adjoining bill
Stares sharply at the sky;
How much further will you rest
Before you opt to fly?

So little time is left to me,
I cannot linger long,
Should you decline to show yourself,
Please let me hear your song.

No hint of sound escapes your bill,
Nor does a feather twitch,
You sit stock-still ignoring me,
While I crouch in my ditch.

At last you stir and stand upright,
But what a great let-down,
Instead of being mauve or pink,
You're merely black and brown.

You slip away beyond my sight,
I've had my final view,
Forever printed on my mind,
Your bill of cyan blue.

Zebu[1]

Zebu! A name so redolent of power,
Indians would regard them as divine,
Here in Madagascar they constitute the dower,
A measure of your wealth compared to mine.

Zebu! They might be riches to a man,
It's such a shame they look like dowdy lumps,
Some of them are brindle, others of them tan,
With, on their backs, extraordinary humps.

Zebu! You find them all across the land,
Forests have been cleared to let them graze,
The pasture lacks nutrition, much of it is sand,
How sad it is they cannot feed on maize.

Zebu! They're scrawny but so strong,
They pull a cart or plough without a break;
With all that mighty effort they do not last for long
And end up in a pot as stewing steak.

1 Hump-backed cattle that are also
  found in number in India

Black Rocks*

You rest within the forest in a quiet and sheltered place,
Buttressed by large rocks from wind and rain;
You earned the lasting comfort of your coffin's close embrace,
A martyr while you breathed to stress and pain.

Who brought you to these sandy shores two hundred years ago?
It could have been French pirates or the Dutch;
What distant land they stole you from the world will never know,
Or who it was that loved you and how much.

You came to Nosy Mangabe[1] as one of many slaves,
Some due to be transported far away;
The others were denied the chance to die among the waves,
Condemned by man's cruel hand to timeless stay.

You would have cut down massive trees and hauled them to the ships,
The source of untold wealth to those you served;
They broke your fragile courage using rustic flails and whips,
Contrived to keep you thoroughly unnerved.

Your manly strength sustained you till you had no more to give,
Then some disease provoked your liberty;
There is no record left to us of when you ceased to live,
The smallest hint of what your name might be.

Your fellow slaves who mourned you put your body in a pit,
Where they were laid beside you in their turn;
When more enlightened men arrived, the skeletons were split,
Revered as missing ancestors, we learn.

They placed you in a coffin which they dragged far up a trail,
Until you reached an outcrop called Black Rocks;
Some men with flags broke into song and girls knelt low to wail,
Your coffin was secured on granite blocks.

I came across that coffin as I trudged up Mangabe
In vain pursuit of aye-aye[2] gnawing bark;
My torch revealed a modest board that told me where you lay –
I paid my silent homage in the dark.

Although you died in slavery your spirit wanders free,
It touched me as I hurtled down a vine,
For while my five companions said my saviour was a tree,
I'm sure your ghostly hand was grasping mine.

1 A beautiful island off the northern coast of Madagascar
2 The largest nocturnal lemur, it is undoubtedly one of the
   weirdest looking creatures on the planet

The Frigatebird[1]

How many worlds have you explored,
Then gauged what each was worth?
You might have glimpsed Gondwanaland[2]
Or Africa's new birth,
A time when pterodactyls[3] flew,
When mammoths[4] strode the Earth.

Within the late Cretaceous age[5]
This island's day first dawned;
You must have flown in virgin sky
To view the life it spawned,
Fresh forest bursting through the rock,
Most lush but some parts thorned.

What ancient marvels did you see
When soaring past this coast?
Of all our Eocene[6] ancestors
Which one impressed you most?
Perhaps old Daubentonia[7],
The aye-aye's[8] giant ghost.

You watched the treescape evanesce
Soon after man arrived,
The forest growth was slashed and burned
And nothing large survived,
The smaller remnants struggled on
But mostly ducked and dived.

And now you check my every move
Upon this coral beach;
I gaze up at your silhouette
So far beyond my reach;
What wisdom I could draw from you
If you had power to teach.

You lived through all the aeons spent
In fashioning this land;
Now in the blinking of Time's eye
You find it stripped to sand;
What message do you have for us
That we will understand?

1 An enormous piratical seabird which looks like a
   relic from our prehistoric past
2 A huge supercontinent that covered most of the
   Southern Hemisphere about 200 million years ago
3 Winged dinosaurs
4 Ancient ancestors of the elephant
5 A period of geological time approximately 143
   to 65 million years ago
6 The Eocene epoch lasted from about 55 to 34
   million years ago
7 An extinct species of aye-aye, about five times
   larger than the present animal; it survived until
   about 1220 AD
8 The largest nocturnal lemur; it is undoubtedly one
   of the weirdest looking creatures on the planet

The Owl House

Introduction

In April 2009 I drove from my temporary South African home in Barrydale (which I describe in the Introduction to 'Contemplative Poems') to Graaff-Reinet, about 300 miles distant in the Great Karoo. Graaff-Reinet is one of South Africa's oldest towns and is replete with buildings of historical interest. It lies close to the Valley of Desolation, a place of vertical cliffs, dolerite columns, unique flora and spectacular views across the plains stretching endlessly below. I spent fruitful hours exploring both town and valley but my principal quest lay elsewhere.

About 30 miles from Graaff-Reinet is another gem, the dorp (village) of Nieu-Bethesda, where the famous playwright Athol Fugard has (or had) a home and where South Africa's most unusual museum is located. This is the 'Owl House', where the reclusive Helen Martins fashioned a dream existence of her own during the middle years of the last century: it retains the power to enchant, indeed captivate, the visitor of today. I was suitably enchanted and captivated! I had been warned by friends in Barrydale, including Fugard's niece, that I would probably find the Owl House and its associated 'Camel Yard' rather depressing as report had it that they were in an advanced state of decay. It therefore came as a very pleasant surprise to discover on my arrival that a cement company had been lending its tangible support to the restoration of the yard and the miscellany of artefacts within it. The Owl House itself was pristine and a short film recorded its history, closure and subsequent restoration. The narrative was racy and irreverent and Helen sparkled into life in my mind.

I took a lot of photographs, which sharpened my memory when I came to write the final nineteen verses of a 'tribute poem' during the coronavirus lockdown in April 2020. Like several other poems of mine I had penned the first verse well in the past, in fact, almost ten years previously. It then lay fallow until a modicum of inspiration struck during my enforced isolation. What better than to take 'the Road to Mecca' (as Athol Fugard described it) and escape to Helen Martins' magical world in Nieu-Bethesda. The poem has some elements that are factual but it is largely a product of my own imagination so it should at best be regarded as 'faction'. To learn more you will have to read the poem!

The Owl House

The Owl House stands empty, alone and unkempt;
Dust masks the well-trodden trails;
Thin walls are creaking with sighs of old ghosts
Who whisper the strangest of tales.

They gasp with dismay at dark days left behind,
Groan for a woman[1] inside,
Kept chained by demands that her father imposed,
No hope of escape 'til he died.

The house was her prison, her only known world,
Except for that painting her dreams;
She broadened horizons by feasting on books,
Religion and travel their themes.

She conjured up lands having magical traits,
Placed far beyond native Karoo;
Imagined the House at the heart of it all,
Attracting choice visitors too.

Pilgrims would come from all parts of the globe
To a Mecca she'd build on her own:
The happiest place they'd encounter on Earth,
Peace beyond any they'd known.

All would be welcome, whenever they came,
No barriers of colour or creed;
The Owl House would give them both shelter and rest,
The comforts that travellers need.

The powers of her father were waning quite fast,
Approaching his ultimate day;
She caged the old lion in part of the House,
Then went on her separate way.

Interior walls were dingy and dull,
No lighting to temper the gloom;
She wanted more mirrors, dappled by sun,
Bright panels throughout every room.

She enlisted the help of a friend in her dorp[2],
A builder with skills she could use;
They started to fashion some tiles for the walls,
Crushed bottles of different hues.

Some panels were yellow, others were red,
Still others were translucent green;
She polished them 'til they sparkled with life,
Glittered with eye-catching sheen.

Mirrors with shapes of the moon and the stars
Reflected new jewels on the walls,
Postcards and pictures and clothing on pegs,
Rich blankets and colourful shawls.

She carved owls by the dozen, figurines too,
Completed this phase of her scheme:
The owl was her symbol of wisdom divine;
Enchantment that gilded her dream.

Next she embarked on converting the yard
To her Promised Land set in the East,
A place of convergence for prophet and king,
Crusader and load-bearing beast.

She'd have supplicant Christians, Muslims in prayer,
Perhaps a sage Buddhist or two,
There'd be camels aplenty transporting her guests
While they traversed the arid Karoo.

She quickly recruited a jack-of-all-trades,
A coloured man³ shunned in his town;
They were intimate friends through bountiful years,
Her very first pilgrim was brown.

They crafted fine tableaux from wire and cement,
Embellished by bottles they chipped,
Scenes from the Bible and Omar Khayyam;
They whittled, they chiselled, they stripped.

The small yard was teeming with camels and owls,
Brick needles and pyramids too:
She drained all her assets pursuing her dream;
Fulfilment was pulling her through.

No longer were strangers encouraged to call;
Instead she drove people away,
Happy alone in the realm she had made,
Her companions those moulded in clay.

She dwelt in great peace 'til time took its toll,
Her eyesight was now fading fast;
All was quite dark in the world she'd contrived,
The journey was over at last.

She swallowed some poison to hasten the end,
Succumbed in most terrible pain:
The Owl House conclusively shut tight its doors;
When would they re-open again?

1 Helen Martins (1897–1976)
2 The remote village of Nieu-Bethesda in the Great Karoo
3 Koos Malpas, who remained with Helen Martins until
   her death

Appendix

Supplementary notes
on selected poems

Notes on 'The African Sun'

Although 'The African Sun' can be regarded as gentle and
whimsical, lamenting my failure, when deep into adulthood,
to rekindle childhood joys, it took me almost 25 years to
complete it! The first four verses flowed fairly easily from
my pen but I then became stuck. I had a tolerably decent
beginning to the poem but no real inkling of how to complete
it to my satisfaction. So it lay fallow for a quarter of a century.
Then, after a period of nine years without a visit to Southern
Africa (save for a brief sojourn in Cape Town), I ventured
to Barrydale in the Little Karoo and found a measure of
inspiration while relaxing among the hills that surround this
lovely village. It was not profound. I simply accepted the
reality that the Africa of my youth could never be the same
as the Africa of today because both Africa and I had changed
with the passage of time: it was futile to think otherwise.
I then composed the final four verses of 'The African Sun'
to reflect that reality.

Notes on 'Umbrella Tree'

The title of the book is drawn from this poem for two reasons. Firstly, the umbrella tree is a distinctive symbol of Africa and my poetry is almost exclusively African in its subject-matter. Secondly, 'umbrella' is a term frequently used to cover a broad range of topics having a common theme. Here the common theme is Africa and the topics range from experiences with elephants to laments for my former homeland of Zimbabwe.

The poem 'Umbrella Tree' reflects the difficulties one often experiences when moving away from one's established zone of comfort. It is always tempting to seek pastures new or the brighter lights or a greater degree of independence. However, it is invariably the reality that the pastures are arid, that the lights are harsh, blinding spotlights and that independence casts one loose from established support. This is not only true for individuals but also for countries, as witness the present plight of Zimbabwe. Ultimately one craves the sanctuary of the known, the familiar and the trusted, imperfect though they may be – and the comfort of darkness, where one can dream undisturbed.

Notes on 'Home'

In 1966 I was fortunate enough to obtain a Rhodes Scholarship to study at Oxford University and left Rhodesia for what turned out to be the final time the following year. When I eventually went back to Salisbury (soon to be Harare) on business in April 1980, the country had been transformed into the newly independent Zimbabwe, with a government of national unity blessed with multiple talents, and tourists were flocking back to the Victoria Falls, game reserves and eastern highland resorts. I had missed thirteen years of UDI (Unilateral Declaration of Independence) and the concomitant international isolation, sanctions and 'war of liberation'.

I became reacquainted with close friends from school, enjoyed the delights of the bush and generally felt I had returned home. But not having shared the pain of the period of strife and armed struggle with my former countrymen, I quickly realised that I did not truly 'belong' and my poem 'Home' records that stark realization. Of all my poems, this is the most personal, with the possible exception of 'The Search', which is a lament for my failure to 'communicate' with my late brother David when I visited his final resting place in the Warren Hills close to Harare.

Notes on the Elephants Trilogy

I have had many wonderful trips into the African bush, particularly in Zimbabwe, and there are numerous incidents involving a variety of animals about which I have written poems, primarily in 'Matilda visits Luangwa'. But the events recounted in the Elephants trilogy will always hold a special place in my memory – and heart. Of all the magnificent animals in Africa, the elephant is my clear favourite; physically imposing and constantly compelling attention and respect, yet surprisingly tolerant of, and gentle towards, humans when they do not feel threatened.

Each tale in the trilogy is true in the smallest detail yet I can honestly attest that never once was I unduly concerned by the proximity of the elephants I describe, whether it be while I was dozing on the ground, sluicing my canoe in the water or pushing my way through an assembly of young bulls to my sleeping accommodation. Although it seems scarcely credible, on each occasion the elephants arrived unnoticed; when they choose to they can move so quietly that you do not hear them.

The nocturnal escapade described in 'Elephants' took place at an upland camp (formerly a private hunting lodge) located in a remote part of the Hwange National Park, just south of the Victoria Falls. The various incidents referred to in 'More Elephants' all occurred during an extended trek in the Chizarira gorges in search of taita falcons. The encounter in 'Elephants Again' occupied a few memorable minutes of a canoe safari along the Zambezi River in the vicinity of the Mana Pools Reserve.

Notes on 'Chapungu'

In 1985 I joined three Zimbabwean friends (two of whom I had known since my early schooldays) on an expedition to Chizarira to check whether or not taita falcons were still breeding in the system of deep gorges that are the principal feature of this extremely remote National Park. The expedition lasted a week and the heat and terrain were gruelling but the scenery, companionship and spirit of adventure made it a trip that I would never forget.

We did not see another human being the entire time we spent in Chizarira but we did witness a pair of taita falcons flying very close to us and also admired a host of other wildlife, including numerous black rhino, which were plentiful in the area. I have described the expedition in some detail in the poem 'More Elephants' which can be found elsewhere in this book.

I have never returned to the Chizarira gorges except in my dreams, the most graphic of which is described in 'Chapungu'. This particular dream, which began very benignly with my being transported thousands of miles to Chizarira on the wings of a mythical Shona bird [see Footnote 1 to the poem], fairly quickly turned into a nightmare as I became increasingly disillusioned with what I 'found' upon my return. The landscape that so bewitched me in 1985 had been largely laid bare and the wildlife, once so abundant, had been decimated. Never had the maxim "to travel hopefully is better than to arrive" been more graphically illustrated for me.

I must emphasise that the poem is essentially a work of fiction and that my imaginings may be rather darker than the present situation at Chizarira warrants. However, I do accurately reflect at least one depressing truth; the black rhino definitely has been butchered into oblivion.

Notes on 'Black Rocks'

Madagascar was a country that was tarnished by the slave trade. I must confess that this was a subject about which I knew very little until a visit in 2007 to the beautiful island of Nosy Mangabe in the north east of the country provoked a strong interest. The object of that visit was to find the aye-aye, the largest of the nocturnal lemurs and one of the strangest creatures on Earth. At the turn of this century the species was feared to be virtually extinct, Nosy Mangabe being one of its few remaining 'strongholds', but recent evidence suggests that it is distributed more widely throughout Madagascar than originally thought and its numbers may be reasonably healthy.

The references in 'Black Rocks' to the treatment of slaves while they were alive, their consignment to pits on death and the reverent reburial of their skeletons by more enlightened generations in the latter part of the nineteenth century are based on the factual research that I conducted upon my return from Madagascar to London. However, what inspired me to write the poem was the experience of sitting beside a slave's simple coffin at a small cemetery (Black Rocks) high in the hills of the island towards the top of a steep, rugged and root-ridden trail. I wondered, in particular, where the slave might originally have come from, who his loved ones might have been and why he was left to work and die in Nosy Mangabe, rather than being transported to some distant land.

Later the same day, after a fruitless search for the aye-aye in pitch darkness (I subsequently saw the animal elsewhere in Madagascar), my companions and I arrived at Black Rocks again. About fifty yards beyond this spot I nearly came to grief when I placed my right foot on what seemed to be a solid rock at the edge of the trail and it broke away, causing me to lurch sideways. I uttered a cry like Tarzan and, in falling, managed to grab a long lianna (vine) which mercifully held my weight as I swung around and located terra firma again. There was a twenty foot drop beneath me while I was airborne. I would like to think that it was the slave's friendly spirit that guided my hand to the vine and ensured it was strong enough to support me!

Printed in Great Britain
by Amazon

44374078R00059